ປາສະໝາມ

ໂດຍ: ໄມກາ ແລະ ໂບຣາ ເມ

Library For All Ltd.

ອົງການ Library For All ແມ່ນອົງການທີ່ບໍ່ຫວັງຜົນກຳໄລ ທີ່ມີພັນທະກິດທີ່ຈະເຮັດໃຫ້ທຸກຄົນ
ສາມາດເຂົ້າເຖິງແຫຼ່ງຄວາມຮູ້ ຜ່ານບະອັດຕະກຳຫ້ອງສະໝຸດດິຈິຕອນ.
ເຂົ້າເບິ່ງລາຍລະອຽດເພີ່ມເຕີມທີ່: libraryforall.org

ປາສະທານ

ຈັດພິມຄັ້ງທຳອິດໃນປີ 2018. ແປ ແລະ ຈັດພິມໃນ ສປປ ລາວ ປີ 2019.

ຈັດພິມໂດຍ: ອົງການ Library For All
ອີເມວ: info@libraryforall.org
URL: libraryforall.org

ປຶ້ມພາສາລາວເຫຼັ້ມນີ້ ຖຶກສະໜັບສະໜູນໂດຍການຮ່ວມມືຂອງ

ປາສະທານ
ໄມກາ ແລະ ໂບຣາ ເນ
ISBN: 978-9932-09-067-9
SKU00839

ປາສະຫຼາມເປັນປາຊະນິດໜຶ່ງ.
ພວກມັນອາໄສຢູ່ໃນທະເລທົ່ວໂລກ.

ມີປາສະໝາມໝາກໝາຍຂະໜົດ.

ປາສະຫວາມກໍ່ບ້ອຍກໍ່ສຸດແມ່ນ
<u>ປາສະຫລາມ ດາຍແລບເທິນ.</u>
ເຈົ້າສາມາດ ຈັບມັນໄວ້ໃນມ໌ໄດ.

ປາສະຫງາມທີ່ໄວທີ່ສຸດແມ່ນ
ປາສະຫງາມທູສັ້ນ ຊື່ວ່າ
ມາໂກ.

ປາສະທູາມມາໂກມີຂະໜາດໃຂ່ຍກ່ວາ
ປາສະທູາມ ດາບແລບເກີບ.

ປາສະໝາມສ່ອນໝ້າຍມິແຂ້ໝ້າຍແຖວ. ແຂ້ວຂອງປາສະໝາມມາໂກມິຄວາມຄົມໝ້າຍ.

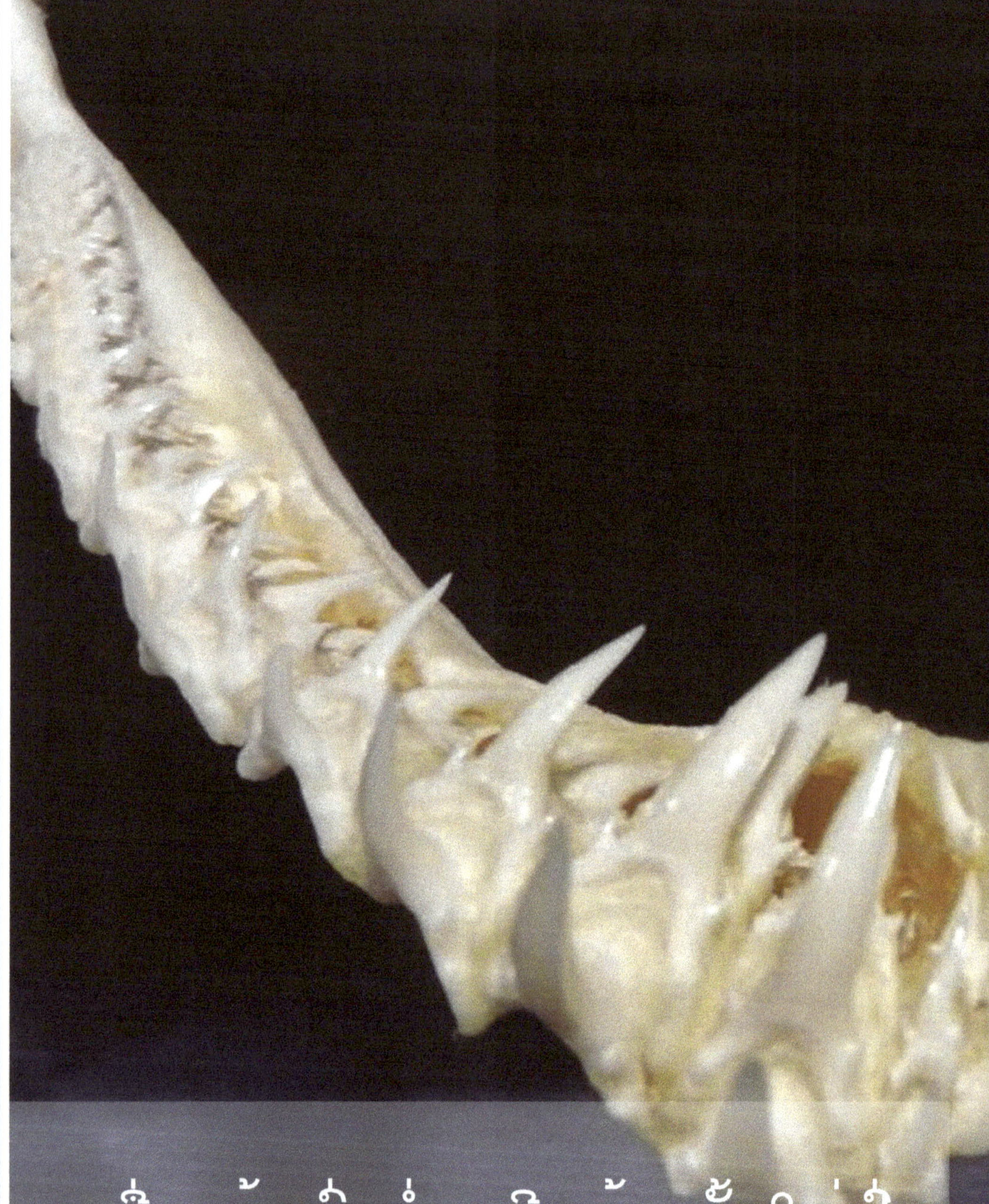

ເມື່ອແຂ້ວຫຼຸບໄປ່ຈະມີ ແຂ້ວເຫຼື້ມໃໝ່ງໆ
ຂຶ້ນມາແຫນບທີ່.

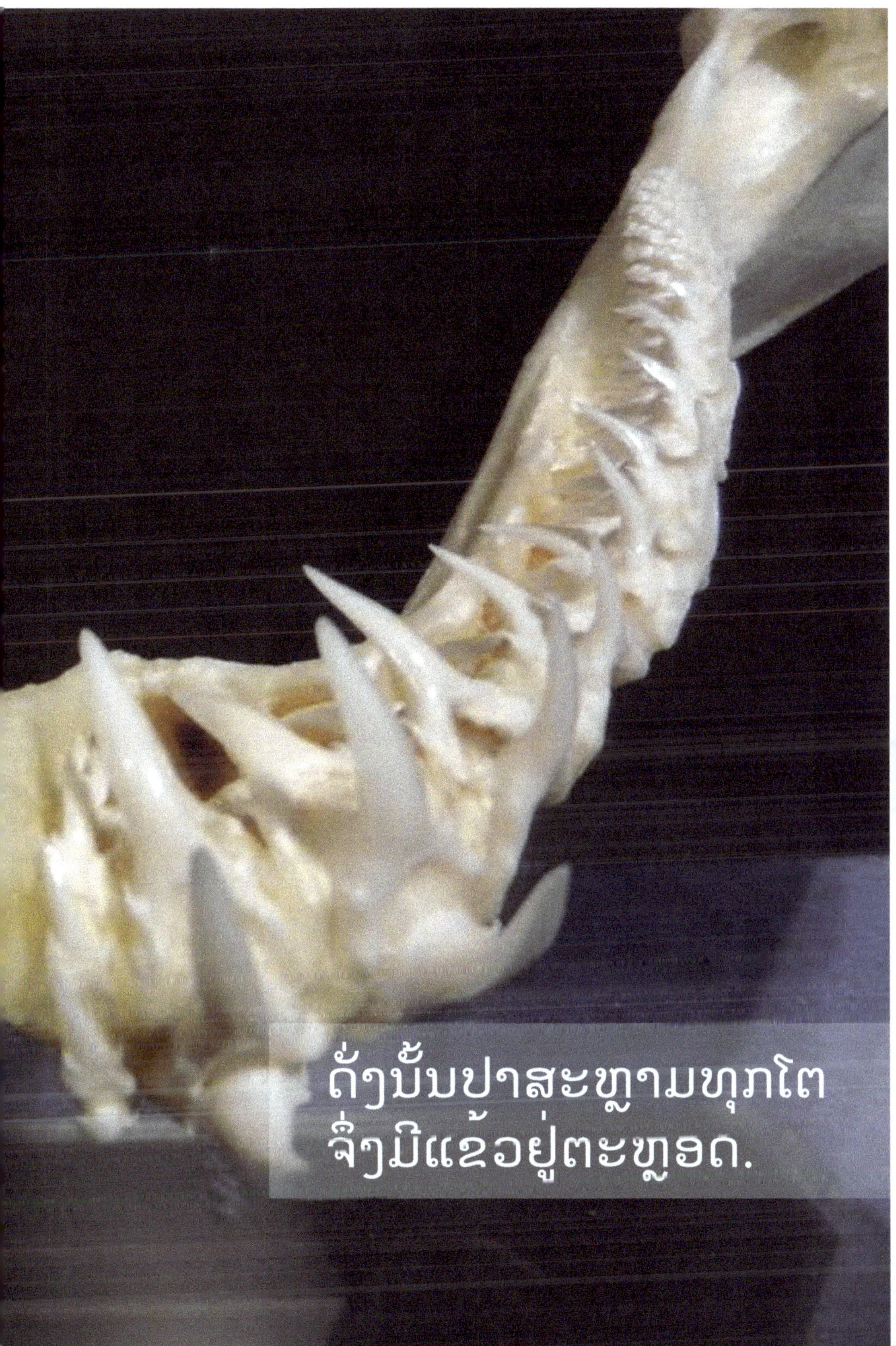

ຄັ້ງນັ້ນປາສະໝ້າມທຸກໂຕ
ຈຶ່ງມິແຂ້ວຢູ່ຕະໝ້ອດ.

ປາສະຫຼາມຂາວໃຫຍ່ ແມ່ນ
ປາສະຫຼາມທີ່ເປັນອັນຕະລາຍ
ທີ່ສຸດ.

ພວກມັນມີແຂ້ວທີ່ແຫຼມຄົມຫຼາຍ.

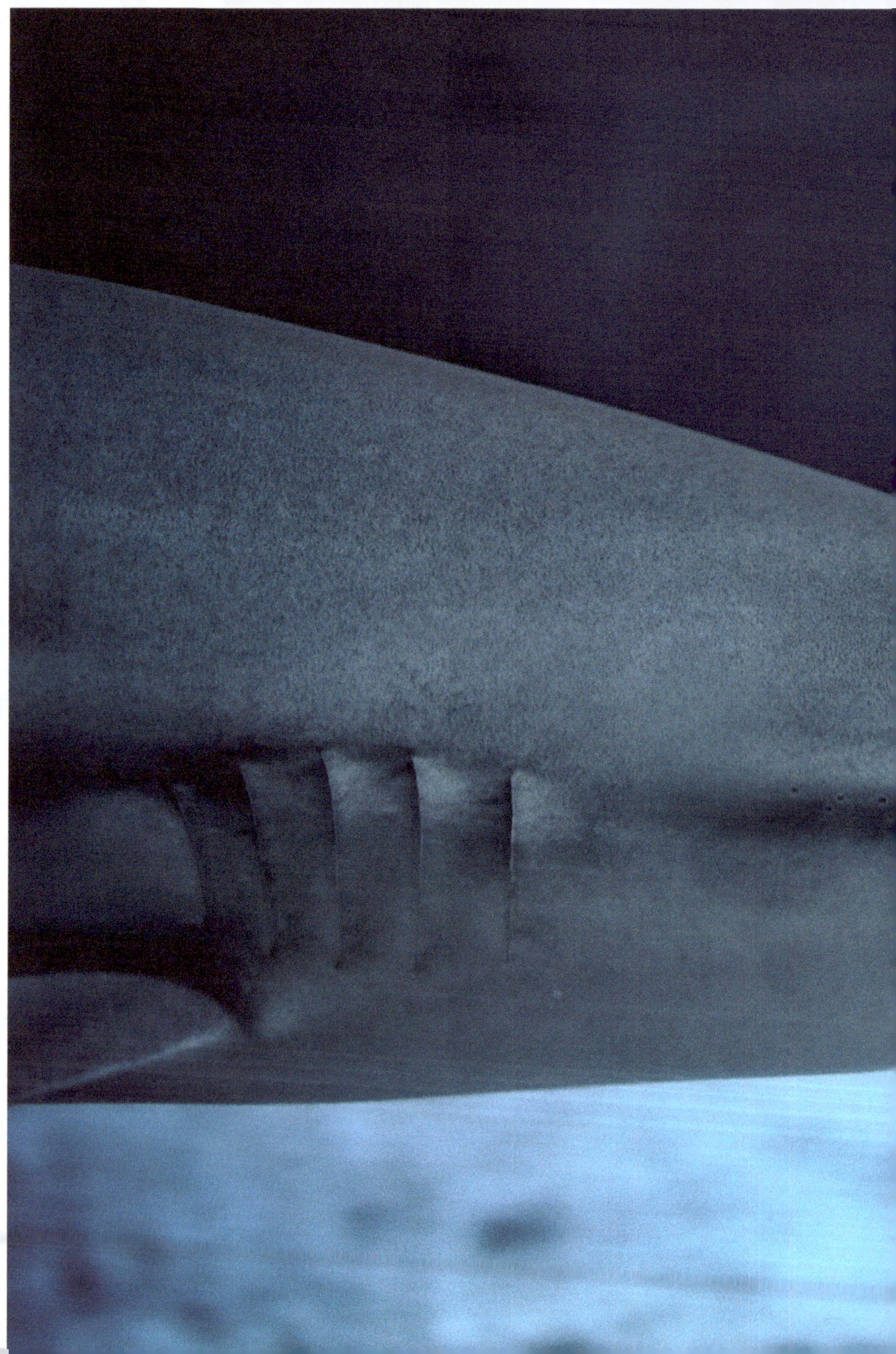

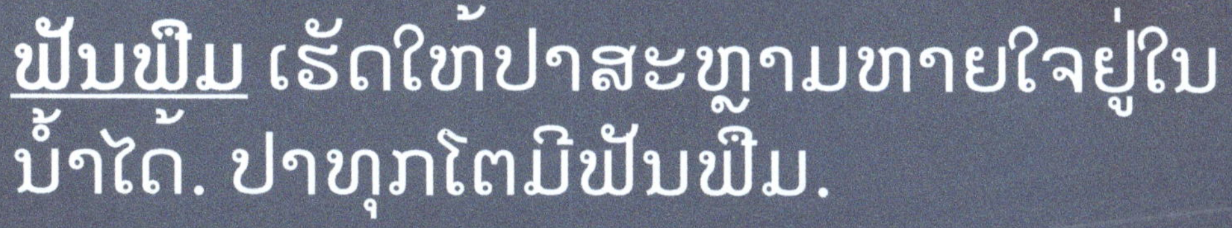
ພັບພຶມ ເຮັດໃຫ້ປາສະຫຼາມຫາຍໃຈຢູ່ໃນ
ນ້ຳໄດ້. ປາທຸກໂຕມີພັບພຶມ.

ປາສະຫຼາມສ່ວນໃຫ່ຍຕ້ອງລອຍນ້ຳ
ເພື່ອຫາຍໃຈ.

ຖ້າພວກມັນຢຸດລອຍນ້ຳ
ພວກມັນກໍ່ຈະຕາຍ.

ປາສະຫຼາມບໍ່ອຍເຫັ້ນອ່າ ລູກປາ.
ເມື່ອພວກມັນເກີດມາພວກມັນຮູ້
ວິທີການລອຍນ້ຳ.

ແມ່ປາສະຫຼາມຈະໂຕໃຫຍ່ກວ່າລູກ
ຂອງມັນ.

ປາສະຫຼາມທີ່ໃຫ່ຍທີ່ສຸດແມ່ນ
ປາສະຫຼາມວານ.

ປາສະຫຼາມອາບບໍ່ເປັນອັນຕະລາຍ. ພວກມັນ ກິນສັ່ງທີ່ມີຊິວິດບ້ອຍໆຢູ່ໃນນ້ຳ ທີ່ເຮົ້ມວ່າ ແພລງຕັນ.

<u>Photo Credits</u>

Domain	Courtesy of	Image	Copyright Holder	Copyright Information	Other Information
Wikimedia Commons	Hermanus Backpackers	Cover	https://commons.wikimedia.org/wiki/File:Great_white_shark_south_africa.jpg	The Wikimedia Foundation owns almost none of the content on Wikimedia sites — the content is owned, instead, by the individual creators of it. However, almost all content hosted on Wikimedia Commons may be freely reused subject to certain restrictions (in many cases). You do not need to obtain a specific statement of permission from the licensor(s) of the content unless you wish to use the work under different terms than the license states.	Content under open content licenses may be reused without any need to contact the licensor(s), but just keep in mind that: • some licenses require that the original creator be attributed; • some licenses require that the specific license be identified when reusing (including, in some cases, stating or linking to the terms of the license); • some licenses require that if you modify the work, your modifications must also be similarly freely licensed; and finally. • Content in the public domain may not have a strict legal requirement of attribution (depending on the jurisdiction of content reuse), but attribution is recommended to give correct provenance.
	Albert kok	Page 1	https://commons.wikimedia.org/wiki/File:Caribbean_reef_shark.jpg		
	Chip Clark/ Smithsonian Institution	Page 2	https://commons.wikimedia.org/wiki/File:Etmopterus_perryi_SI_cr.jpg		
	Mark Conlin, SWFSC Large Pelagics Program	Page 3	https://commons.wikimedia.org/wiki/File:Isurus_oxyrinchus_by_mark_conlin2.JPG		
	Spotty11222	Page 4	https://commons.wikimedia.org/wiki/File:Close_up_of_mako_shark_head_005.jpg		
	Pterantula (Terry Goss)	Page 5	https://commons.wikimedia.org/wiki/File:Great_White_Shark_(14730719119).jpg		
	Happy Little Nomad	Page 11	https://commons.wikimedia.org/wiki/File:Carcharhinus_obscurus_at_Seaworld.jpg		
	Zac Wolf and Stefan	Page 12	https://commons.wikimedia.org/wiki/File:Whale_shark_Georgia_aquarium.jpg		
	Derek Keats	Page 13	https://commons.wikimedia.org/wiki/File:Whale_shark,_Rhincodon_typus,_at_Daedalus_in_the_Egyptian_Red_Sea._(35827412321).jpg		
Flickr	Travis	Page 5	https://www.flickr.com/photos/baggis/6139383927	Our public licenses are intended for use by those authorized to give the public permission to use material in ways otherwise restricted by copyright and certain other rights. Our licenses are irrevocable. Licensors should read and understand the terms and conditions of the license they choose before applying it. Licensors should also secure all rights necessary before applying our licenses so that the public can reuse the material as expected. Licensors should clearly mark any material not subject to the license. This includes other CC-licensed material, or material used under an exception or limitation to copyright.	By using one of our public licenses, a licensor grants the public permission to use the licensed material under specified terms and conditions. If the licensor's permission is not necessary for any reason–for example, because of any applicable exception or limitation to copyright–then that use is not regulated by the license. Our licenses grant only permissions under copyright and certain other rights that a licensor has authority to grant. Use of the licensed material may still be restricted for other reasons, including because others have copyright or other rights in the material. A licensor may make special requests, such as asking that all changes be marked or described. Although not required by our licenses, you are encouraged to respect those requests where reasonable.
	Travelbag Ltd	Page 7	https://www.flickr.com/photos/98585738@N07/10346101216/		

Domain	Courtesy of	Image	Copyright Holder	Copyright Information	Other Information
PixaBay	StockSnap	Page 8	https://pixabay.com/en/nature-water-animals-shark-blue-2570749/	Images and Videos on Pixabay are released under Creative Commons CC0. To the extent possible under law, uploaders of Pixabay have waived their copyright and related or neighboring rights to these Images and Videos. You are free to adapt and use them for commercial purposes without attributing the original author or source. Although not required, a link back to Pixabay is appreciated.	Images and Videos may not be used in a way that shows identifiable persons in a disgraceful light, or to imply endorsement of products and services by depicted persons, brands, and organisations - unless permission was granted. Certain Images or Videos may be subject to additional copyrights, property rights, trademarks etc. and may require the consent of a third party or the license of these rights.
	Wildfaces	Page 9	https://pixabay.com/en/blacktip-hai-dangerous-1294753/		
MaxPixel	N/A	Page 10	http://maxpixel.freegreatpicture.com/Kobia-Whale-Shark-Underwater-Ocean-Fish-Divers-207401	The person who associated a work with this deed has dedicated the work to the public domain by waiving all of his or her rights to the work worldwide under copyright law, including all related and neighboring rights, to the extent allowed by law. You can copy, modify, distribute and perform the work, even for commercial purposes, all without asking permission.	In no way are the patent or trademark rights of any person affected by CC0, nor are the rights that other persons may have in the work or in how the work is used, such as publicity or privacy rights. Unless expressly stated otherwise, the person who associated a work with this deed makes no warranties about the work, and disclaims liability for all uses of the work, to the fullest extent permitted by applicable law. When using or citing the work, you should not imply endorsement by the author or the affirmer.

<u>ປະມວນຄຳສັບ</u>

<u>ປາສະທ່ານ ດາບແລບເທິບ</u>
ເປັນປາສະທ່ານທີ່ບ້ອຍທີ່ສຸດໃນໂລກ.

<u>ຟັບຟິນ</u>
ເປັນອະໄວຍະວະທີ່ຊ່ວຍໃຫ້ປາສະທ່ານ ແລະ
ປາຂະນິດອື່ນໆຫາຍໃຈຢູ່ໃນນ້ຳໄດ້.

<u>ປາສະທ່ານຂາວໃຫ່ຍ</u>
ເປັນສະທ່ານທີ່ອັນຕະລາຍທີ່ສຸດໃນໂລກ.

<u>ລູກປາ</u>
ລູກປາສະທ່ານ

<u>ແພລງຕັນ</u>
ວັດຂະພິດ ແລະ ສັດນ້ອຍໆທີ່ລອຍຢູ່ໃນນ້ຳ.

<u>ປາສະທ່ານ ທູສັ້ນ ມາໂກ</u>
ເປັນປາສະທ່ານທີ່ໄວທີ່ສຸດໃນໂລກ.

<u>ປາສະທ່ານອານ</u>
ເປັນປາສະທ່ານທີ່ໃຫ່ຍທີ່ສຸດໃນໂລກ.

ກ່ຽວກັບຜູ້ຂຽນ

ໄມກາ ເມ ເປັນຜູ້ອຳນວຍການຝ່າຍເທັກໂນໂລຢີ ໃຫ້ກັບ
Library For All ແລະ ຍັງເຮັດວຽກເປັນທີ່ປຶກສາດ້ານ
ອິບຸກ ໃຫ້ກັບ Digital Public Library of America.
ລາວຫຼຽງໄຫຼ ກ່ຽວກັບການຊ່ວຍເຫຼືອທ້ອງສະໝຸດ
ໃຫ້ມີຄວາມກ້າວໜ້າ ທາງດ້ານໜັງສືໄປທົ່ວໂລກ. ໄມກາໄດ້ຮັບ
ປະລິນຍາຕີຈາກມະຫາວິທະຍາໄລໂຄໂລຣາໂດ ແລະ JD
ຈາກໂຮງຮຽນກົດໝາຍຮາເວິດ.

ໂນຣາ ເມ ຢູ່ຂັ້ນຮຽນປີທີ່ສາມຂອງໂຮງຮຽນ ແຊັງ ໂຄລຸມບາ ໃນ
ດູຣັງໂກ ລັດໂຄໂລຣາໂດ. ລາວມັກການອ່ານ ແລະ ບົດລາຍງານ
ທຳອິດຂອງລາວ ກ່ຽວກັບປາສະທູງາມໄດ້ສ້າງແຮງບັນດາບໃຈໃຫ້
ກັບໜັງສືເຫຼັ້ມນີ້.

ຂໍ້ມູນທາງບັນນາບຸລິມຂອງຫໍສະໝຸດແຫ່ງຊາດ

ໄມກາ

ປາສະທູານ 2 / ໂດຍ ໄມກາ ແລະ ໂບຣາ ເມ. -- ວຽງຈັນ :
ມັກອານ, 2020

34 ໜ້າ : ພາບປະກອບສີ ; 29 ຊມ
1. ປາສະທູານ
2. ວັນນະກຳສຳລັບເດັກ
I. ຊື່ເລື່ອງ

597.3 – dc21
ISBN 978-9932-09-067-9
ເລກທະບຽນພິມຈຳໜ່າຍ: ຕາມທບ 150 ພຈ 23032020

ທ່ານມັກປຶ້ມເຫຼັ້ມນີ້ບໍ່?

ທ່ານສາມາດອ່ານປຶ້ມແບບນີ້ໄດ້ເພີ່ມເຕີມ
ທີ່ຜະລິດໂດຍອົງການ Library For All

ອົງການ Library For All ຜະລິດສື່ການອ່ານ ທີ່ມີຄຸນນະພາບ
ເໝາະສົມກັບວັດທະນະທຳເພື່ອການສຶກສາ ໂດຍນຳໃຊ້ນະວັດຕະ
ກຳແອັບພິເຖຊັ່ນຫ້ອງສະໝຸດແບບອິນຊກ. ພວກເຮົາເຮັດວຽກຮ່ວມ
ກັບນັກຂຽນໃນທ້ອງຖິ່ນ, ຄູອາຈານ, ທີ່ປຶກສາດ້ານວັດທະນະທຳ,
ລັດຖະບານ ແລະ ອົງການຈັດຕັ້ງທີ່ບໍ່ຂຶ້ນກັບລັດຖະບານ
ເພື່ອມອບຄວາມສຸກຂອງການອ່ານໃຫ້ແກ່ເດັກນ້ອຍ ທຸກໆແຫ່ງ.

ມາອ່ານນຳກັບເທາະ!
libraryforall.org